Copyright © 2022 Tall Girl Publishing

All rights reserved. This book, or any parts, may not be reproduced in any form without written permission from the publisher.

"Lemonade Lilli" is a work of fiction. This story is original and all characters are products of the author's imagination. Any correlations to real life are purely coincidental.

ISBN: 978-1958023-10-5 (Hard Cover)
ISBN: 978-1958023-06-8 (Paperback)
ISBN: 978-1958023-07-5 (eBook)

Library of Congress Control Number:
         9781958023068

Cover design by Joan Enockson
Illustrations by Jennifer Hansen

JUV006000,   JUV009000,   JUV013070,   JUV014000,
JUV024000,   JUV039050,   JUV039200,   JUV039090,
JUV039220

First printing, 2022

Tall Girl Publishing
Laurens, IA

https://www.joanenockson.com
joanenockson6@gmail.com

Dedication

I dedicate this book to the memory of my dad (1942-2021).

Sid Tiemersma was a dairy farmer in Northwest Washington State. Some of my best childhood memories were of times spent following him, or my grandfather, as they worked in the shop, barns, milk house, or fields.

Growing up on a farm was wonderful, and I will always cherish those memories.

Lemonade Lilli

Written by: Joan Enockson
Illustrated by: Jennifer Hansen

*Jace & Jaxson,
  Work for what you want!*
  Joan Enockson

Chapter 1

Lilli sat on the front steps, lost in thought. She and her older brother, Larry, were staying at their grandparents' house while their parents were on vacation. They lived a few miles from town on a farm, and Lilli loved staying with her grandparents. Not only were there fun things to do, three of her best friends lived on the same road! Today, however, there was an idea trying to take shape in her mind, but it wasn't quite there yet. The farm's orange cat, Mother Kitty, tried her best to get Lilli's attention by rubbing her long soft fur against Lilli's legs, but Lilli didn't seem to notice.

"Hmmm . . ." she muttered to herself.

Lilli was thinking about a conversation that she had overheard Larry having with his friends. Larry was in high school, and he and his friends were talking about money. They were always interested in how to get more of it. While listening to the boys' discussion, Lilli soon picked up on the fact that money was important to have if you wanted to go somewhere with your friends or buy something you wanted—and she wanted plenty of things!

Grandpa, on the other hand, talked about money differently. He always said that you should be "saving money, giving money, and spending money." Lilli wasn't sure how that worked, but there was one thing she was sure of: She wanted to earn some money!

"I need to talk to Grandpa," she told Mother Kitty.

Lilli took a moment to pet the fluffy orange cat before standing up and heading toward the shop. She walked down the sidewalk, through the yard gate, and across the farmyard. Lilli knew Grandpa would be there; he was always fixing this or sharpening that. "A farmer's work is never done," he would say.

Chapter 2

Before Lilli entered the shop, she could hear the sound of the grinder spinning. When it made contact with metal, sparks flew like shooting stars, bouncing off the cement floor before disappearing forever. Lilli loved watching Grandpa sharpen blades with the grinder. She considered it her own personal fireworks display.

The shop was actually an old garage attached to another garage and a couple of open stalls. It smelled of oil and grease and was filled with all sorts of mechanical parts. Small boxes, filled with many different sizes of nails, screws, nuts, and bolts lined one wall. Another wall was lined with pegboard and on it hung various hammers, saws, and practically any sort of tool you could imagine. The collection of tools was organized neatly according to size.

Lilli walked into the garage, found a pair of safety glasses, and watched as Grandpa worked. She knew better than to interrupt him, so she waited patiently for him to finish while enjoying her fireworks. She thought once more about wanting to make money and just knew Grandpa would be the one to help her.

Grandpa took his time sharpening the lawn mower blade, making sure it was as sharp as he could get it. He took pride in his work and would always say, "The work's still there until it gets done." Grandpa was full of sayings, and it wasn't hard to understand the wisdom in them.

The fireworks display eventually ended and Grandpa flipped up his face shield.

"Hello there, Lilli Bean."

Lilli couldn't remember a time when Grandpa didn't call her Lilli Bean. He was the only one who called her that, and it made her feel special.

"Well, did you come out here to learn more about sharpening?" Grandpa chuckled, knowing Lilli had something else on her mind.

"Grandpa, Larry keeps talking about making money. He says that money is how you get things."

Grandpa grabbed a nearby five-gallon bucket, turned it upside down across from Lilli, and sat down. "Well, Larry is right. Money is how you are able to buy things, but you have to earn it."

"Then I want to earn money, too!" Lilli said firmly. "Grandpa, do you know how I can do that?"

"Well, you are a bit too young to have a big job, but I think we can come up with a good way for you to make some money. My stomach says it's coffee time, so let's go to the house and do some thinking." Grandpa put his equipment away, Lilli did likewise, and started walking briskly back to the house. Lilli skipped behind him, her long red ponytail bouncing up and down, excited that she was going to start making some money!

Chapter 3

Lilli and Grandpa sat down at the kitchen table, where there was already a plate of banana bread sitting out next to a hot cup of coffee. Grandpa retrieved a yellow pad of paper and, between bites and sips, wrote at the top of the paper *Lilli's Business Ideas*.

"Now, Lilli, the important thing about making money is making sure you can do the work and are as professional as possible."

Lilli watched as Grandpa wrote a column on the paper labeled *Ideas*. "But how do ideas make money?" Lilli asked.

Grandpa chuckled and began to explain, "Well, Lilli, we have to come up with an idea to make money that matches something you can do."

Lilli rubbed her chin as she began to think. "Perhaps I could sell my dolls!" She quickly realized she would miss her dolls. *That idea wouldn't work,* she thought.

Lilli hopped down from her chair and walked to the counter to retrieve a glass from the cupboard. "I need something to drink. This is hard work, coming up with ideas." She opened the fridge and pulled out the lemonade she had made yesterday, and then poured herself a glass to drink. As the glass started to fill up, Lilli was struck with an idea. "Lemonade!" she suddenly shouted.

Grandpa looked up and said, "That's a great idea, Lilli!" He wrote down his idea for the business name, *Lemonade Lilli.* Lilli sat back down at the table, eager to get started.

"First, we need to come up with your business model and make you a record book," Grandpa told her, flipping to a new blank sheet of paper.

"Well, the business model is to make money!" Lilli chimed in, thinking she had solved all the problems.

"That is the goal, but we need to look at a lot of different things here, Lilli," said Grandpa as he wrote. "We need to figure out how much money you will need to buy your lemonade supplies, how much you are going to sell each cup for, and how many you want to try and sell in a day to make a profit. We also need to build you a lemonade stand and figure out where you should set up your business."

Lilli was shocked at how much thought had to go into a business idea! She collected her own sheet of paper and a pencil and thought about how she could keep track of her sales. After a few moments, her face lit up and she began sketching out her idea. Likewise, Grandpa was creating some sketches of his own.

Chapter 4

Both were singularly focused on their sketching as Grandma walked in. "What's going on here?" she asked curiously as she looked over their shoulders.

"I'm going to make money, and Grandpa is helping me!" Lilli volunteered.

"Oh, he is, is he?" Grandma teased.

Grandpa looked up from his sketch and replied, "We have a business entrepreneur on our hands, and she is motivated!"

Lilli lifted up her paper to show her grandparents. "Look! I drew lots of lemons. My plan is to color one lemon for each glass of lemonade I sell, and at the bottom I can write how much I'm selling it for and how much money I make. This way, if I get busy with a lot of customers, I can add it up later."

"That sounds like a good plan," said Grandpa.

"How can I help?" Grandma asked.

"Can you help me with my lemonade supplies?"

"I sure can." Grandma grabbed a stack of papers from a pile at the end of the counter and took a seat next to Lilli.

Lilli noticed that Grandma had brought over the coupon pages from the newspaper. She turned to Lilli and said, "This time of year, lemonade is usually on sale."

Lilli flipped over her paper and started making a list of supplies: *lemonade mix, cups, money box, sales record book, yellow crayons.* She showed Grandma her list. "Did I miss anything?" she asked.

Grandma looked it over carefully. "That list looks pretty good to me. However, we will also need the beverage cooler from the storage closet. Why don't you run down and get it? I'll look for coupons."

Lilli raced to the storage closet and found Grandma's big red beverage cooler. It had a spigot on the bottom of it, which made it easy to pour drinks. You just had to push the button!

She made her way back to the kitchen, bumping into the doorway as she entered.

"That cooler is about as big as you!" Grandpa teased. "Set that on the counter and come see what I've been working on."

Lilli set the cooler on the counter and skipped over to Grandpa. He turned his notepad so she could see what he had drawn. "Wow!" Lilli said, her eyes growing wide. Grandpa had drawn a picture of her very own lemonade stand! She felt proud seeing her name on the top of it: *Lemonade Lilli*.

Grandpa pushed his chair back, stood up, and said, "I'll go find Larry, and he and I can get to work building it. I know there's plenty of wood in the scrap pile out behind the shop."

Lilli threw her arms around him and said, "Thank you, Grandpa!"

"You're welcome, Lilli Bean," he said, hugging her back. He then walked towards the door, found his hat, and headed out to find Larry.

Chapter 5

Lilli sat down again next to Grandma. "Did you find any coupons?"

"I sure did," replied Grandma. "These coupons will help you with your bottom line."

Lilli gave her a confused look. "My bottom line?"

"Your bottom line is how much money you will actually make. You must take the total amount of money you collect from your customers minus the cost of your supplies. By using coupons to buy your supplies, you can get your supplies for a lower cost—or a discount—and improve your bottom line."

"Ohhh," said Lilli, nodding with understanding. "I get it now."

Grandma wrote a number down and showed it to Lilli. "This is what your supplies will cost. Do you have that amount saved?"

Lilli thought for a second before leaving the table and bounding upstairs. She ran to her dresser, found the quart Mason jar with all of her money she had stashed away, and brought it back down to the kitchen. She dumped it out on the table and together, she and Grandma counted it.

"You are a few dollars short," said Grandma. "But those coupons really helped you! Why don't you ask your grandpa if he has a few dollars to make up the difference?"

Lilli beamed. She was so excited! "Can we go to the store now?" she asked.

"Absolutely!" replied Grandma, standing up and grabbing her purse. "Go find your grandpa, and I'll meet you at the truck."

Lilli grabbed her money and went to find Grandpa. As she approached the shop, she could hear the uneven banging of hammers against wood. Lilli stopped when she saw the framework of her soon-to-be lemonade stand. It was one thing to have a great idea but a completely different thing to see your idea becoming real!

Larry noticed Lilli and stopped hammering. "Hey, kiddo, what do you think so far?"

"I love it!" cried Lilli, clapping her hands.

Grandpa stopped hammering, too, and asked, "Do you have your supply list all ready to go?"

"I sure do, but I'm a couple dollars short. Grandma sent me out to ask you if you had a few to spare. Do you?" asked Lilli hopefully.

Grandpa chuckled, found his wallet, and pulled out a couple of dollars. "Let me be the first to donate to your business." Grandpa placed the dollars in Lilli's hand as her face lit up with excitement. "See the importance of giving?" he said with a wink.

Lilli squealed and ran to the truck, calling over her shoulder, "Thank you, Grandpa!"

Grandma was already waiting in the truck for her. As Lilli climbed in, Grandma turned the key and the engine roared to life. Lilli could hardly sit still—her idea was becoming a reality!

Chapter 6

After a quick trip to the store, Lilli ran inside with her bag of supplies and started making lemonade as fast as she could.

It didn't take her long to make several gallons, and she put each batch in the fridge to cool down. Lilli then ran back outside to Grandpa and Larry, who were still working hard on her lemonade stand.

"I'm ready to start making some money, Grandpa!" Lilli stated with confidence.

"Well, we have a bit more work to do before you're ready to start selling. This stand will need some paint after we're finished, and we still need to decide where you're going to set up business."

Lilli's face fell. She was starting to feel impatient. Lilli wanted to make money now, not work some more. Larry sympathetically patted Lilli on the head and headed back into the house.

"It's quittin' time, Lilli Bean," Grandpa said. "We'll work on it again in the morning. In the meantime, I'm sure your grandma has a fine dinner waiting for us."

Lilli did feel hungry and made her way toward the house. She wished her project would move along faster, but she also trusted Grandpa. He always knew the right thing to do. As she passed through the yard gate, Mother Kitty was there to greet her.

"I'm going to make some money, kitty cat!" said Lilli, skipping the rest of the way to the house.

Chapter 7

As soon as she awoke the next day, Lilli could think of nothing else besides her lemonade stand business—that is, until she smelled Grandma's pancakes! She quickly got dressed and made her way down to the kitchen.

"Are you ready for your big day?" Grandma asked as she set a plate of pancakes in front of her.

"I sure am!" Lilli answered as she covered her pancakes in sticky syrup.

"Your grandpa and Larry already ate and have headed out to put the finishing touches on your lemonade stand. It won't be long now, and then it'll be ready for painting," Grandma said as she poured Lilli some milk.

Lilli finished her breakfast and started to pick up her plate. She couldn't wait to go see her lemonade stand!

"I'll take care of these dishes. You run along," Grandma said with a smile.

Lilli looked gratefully at her grandma and hurried out the door. She was immediately greeted with ringing bike bells coming up the driveway.

Lexie, Carole, and Kaylee were Lilli's best friends. The girls all lived close by to her grandparents' farm, and they loved it when Lilli stayed with them. As they hopped off their bikes and rushed over to the shop, they exclaimed, "Wow!" Lexie couldn't stand not knowing what was going on and immediately asked, "What's this for?"

"I'm going to sell lemonade!" Lilli shouted. The three girls excitedly jumped up and down and began asking a million questions. Lilli answered each one with enthusiasm, grateful to feel excited again.

Carole offered an idea. "We could make signs!"

"We could help sell!" Kaylee contributed.

Lexie looked at the stand and said, "This thing needs paint."

"What a good idea!" Grandpa said with a twinkle in his eye.

Lilli was excited that her friends wanted to help. The four girls went to the house with the plan to look for poster boards and paint. Lilli was surprised to discover the kitchen table already covered in poster boards, markers, paint, brushes, glue, and even glitter!

Grandma stood by the kitchen sink and smiled. "I thought you might come looking for these."

Lilli gave her grandma a huge smile. "You were right! Thanks!"

The girls collected their materials, went outside, and set up their workspace on the spacious front porch. They discussed possible locations for the business and possible ways to get customers to buy Lilli's lemonade. For the next couple of hours, they chatted away and created colorful posters advertising the best lemonade in town!

"You should set up at the tractor dealership!" Carole suggested. "It's just down the road."

"That's a great idea!" Lilli answered. "I bet Larry could take me and my lemonade stand there in his pickup."

Lexi added, "I know lots of places where we could hang these posters. After we're finished making them, Carole, Kaylee, and I could ride our bikes to town and put them up for you."

"That would be great!" With the collective plan taking shape, Lilli's excitement was building again.

Just then, Grandma came out with a plate of cookies. "You girls are working so hard, I thought you might need a break."

The girls eagerly took Grandma up on her offer of homemade chocolate chip cookies and washed them down with the customary glass of milk.

Between delicious, gooey chocolate bites, Lilli informed Grandma of their plan to set up the lemonade stand at the tractor dealership down the road. "That's a great idea," Grandma said, "but we need to ask permission first."

"Oh, I never thought of that," replied Lilli with a hint of concern. "Do you think they'll let us?"

"I don't know," replied Grandma. "It doesn't hurt to ask. The worst thing that could happen is they say 'no', but what that really means is 'next.' " Lilli gave her grandma a confused look. She explained further, "When you get a 'no' from someone, your next step is to go ask someone else."

"So if I can't set up my lemonade stand at the tractor dealership, I just go and ask a different business?"

"Right!" Grandma confirmed. "Why don't you girls ask Larry to drive you down to the dealership while your posters dry? He just came in a little while ago and went upstairs. Girls, you'll need to move your bikes out of the driveway and prop them up against the fence. Oh, when you arrive at the dealership, ask to speak to Mr. Barnham. He's the owner. If he says yes, then you can add the location on to your posters before you post them around town."

Lexie, Carole, and Kaylee went to move their bikes, and Lilli ran upstairs to find Larry, lying on his bed, sketching. "Larry," she begged, "Will you drive me to the tractor dealership?"

"Are you buying a tractor?" he teased.

"No, silly," Lilli chided as she found a nearby pillow and threw it at Larry's head. "I need to ask Mr. Barnham if I can set up my lemonade stand in his parking lot."

She explained her entire plan, and after hearing his sister's excitement, Larry grabbed his truck keys. "Alright, let's go!"

Chapter 8

Lilli quickly grabbed her business plan from the kitchen table before she and her friends made their way outside. They all piled into Larry's truck, eager to get to the dealership. Larry grinned at the four excited faces smiling up at him. *Mr. Barnham is doomed,* he thought. "Make sure you are polite and give Mr. Barnham your best smile," Larry advised.

Larry soon pulled up to the front door of the dealership and the girls spilled out of the truck.

"I'll introduce you to Mr. Barnham, but after that, you do the talking."

"Got it," said Lilli. She was beginning to feel nervous about talking to Mr. Barnham but decided to do as Larry had suggested.

The girls followed Larry inside and watched with anticipation as he walked to a man wearing a green shirt and a baseball cap. Lilli relaxed a bit when she saw that he had kind eyes and a friendly smile.

"Well, hello, Larry, are you finally buying a tractor?" he joked as he extended his hand to shake Larry's.

"Not today, Mr. Barnham," Larry said with a grin, "but my little sister has a business proposition for you." He put his hand behind Lilli's back and gently coaxed her forward. "This is my sister, Lilli."

Lilli took a deep breath, looked up at Mr. Barnham, and gave him her best smile. "Hello, Mr. Barnham. I have started my own business, just like you." She handed him her prized business plan before continuing. "I have my business all planned out. My grandpa and grandma helped me with it."

The seasoned tractor salesman looked over Lilli's plan and was impressed. "You seem to have it all figured out," he said as he handed back the business plan.

"Oh, I do!" exclaimed Lilli.

Mr. Barnham scratched his chin and furrowed his brow, trying to hide his amusement. He could see Lilli was serious and wanted to treat their conversation with respect. He noticed the three other girls with worried looks hiding behind Larry as he waited for Lilli to continue.

"I want to earn some money, so Grandpa helped me come up with an idea to work for it. Grandpa and Larry built me a lemonade stand, and Grandma found coupons so I could improve my bottom line."

Mr. Barnham raised his eyebrows when Lilli mentioned improving her "bottom line." He was once again impressed at the sound business sense she was learning from her grandparents.

Lilli continued, "She took me to the store and I used my very own money to buy supplies! Oh, and my friends helped me to make posters to hang around town."

As if right on cue, the three worried faces peeked out from behind Larry and erupted into big smiles. Mr. Barnham took a quick moment to glance at Larry, who was leaning against the counter, arms folded, grinning from ear to ear with a look in his eyes that seemed to say, *You're doomed.*

Mr. Barnham turned his attention back to Lilli. "What do you need from me?" he asked seriously.

Lilli's face lit up—Mr. Barnham had given her the perfect segue for her next question. "Mr. Barnham, could I set up my lemonade stand in your parking lot this afternoon? You really do have the perfect location," she added with an extra big smile.

Mr. Barnham continued to look serious and asked, "What's in it for me?"

Lilli's face fell. She looked to Larry for help, but he just smiled at her. Lilli thought hard about Mr. Barnham's question. Lexie, Carole, and Kaylee lost their smiles and the worried faces returned.

She suddenly remembered something her grandma always said. Lilli looked up at Mr. Barnham bravely. "My grandma always says that to accomplish something important, it takes a village. I've had a lot of help from my grandpa, grandma, Larry, Lexie, Carole, and Kaylee. You probably had help from a lot of people when you started your business, too." Lilli took a moment to choose her words carefully before continuing. "What if my customers became your customers and your customers became my customers?"

Mr. Barnham couldn't contain himself any longer and allowed his face to break into a smile. He offered his hand to Lilli and said, "I think that is a very good answer, and yes, you have my permission to set up your lemonade stand in my parking lot."

Lilli shook Mr. Barnham's hand and gave him her extra special smile as squeals of delight exploded from the three girls behind her.

"Thank you, Mr. Barnham, I really appreciate it!" replied Lilli, feeling the most excited she had felt all day!

Larry clapped his hands and said, "Well done, little sister. Now, if I remember right, that stand of yours needs paint. Let's go!"

Chapter 9

Everyone scrambled into the pickup again and headed back to the farm. They arrived just as Grandpa was setting out cans of paint.

"Perfect timing!" Grandpa bellowed. "Larry, I'm going to need your artistic touch as soon as Lilli and I give this stand a proper coat of paint." Larry was well-known for his ability to draw and often contributed his artwork to the school newspaper.

"I'll get my sketchpad," he said, walking back to his truck to retrieve it. Larry was never far from his sketchpad; he took it everywhere he went. "You never know when an idea is going to hit you," he would say. Larry put down the tailgate of his truck, hopped up, and got to work.

"Grandpa," Lilli said, "I need to check on our posters first, and then I'll be right back."

"Alright," Grandpa replied. "I'll stir up some of this paint for you and it'll be ready to go when you get back."

The girls grinned and ran back to the house to see if their posters were dry. As they approached, Lilli noticed Grandma, with her hands on her hips, studying the posters.

"It looks like you had some extra help," she said.

"Oh no!" the girls wailed. On every poster were the distinct paw prints left by Mother Kitty.

"Now we have to start over!" Lilli whined.

The girls were on the verge of tears when Grandma interjected, "You know, some businesses have a mascot, don't they? Why don't you make Mother Kitty your mascot? The way I see it, Mother Kitty has given your business her stamp of approval."

Lilli smiled at Grandma's words, and it reminded her of another saying she often heard Grandma use. It also seemed incredibly fitting at this moment, so Lilli said it out loud. "When life gives you lemons . . ." Grandma turned to Lilli, grinned, and said the rest of it along with her, "You make lemonade!"

Everyone laughed and giggled at the irony of the situation, and the few tears that had escaped now became tears of laughter rather than frustration.

"How did it go with Mr. Barnham?" Grandma asked.

"It went great!" Lilli went on to tell Grandma all about her conversation as well as the advice Larry had given her on the way there.

"It sounds like you handled yourself just as a professional businessperson should. I'm very proud of you."

The girls quickly wrote the location and hours of Lilli's business on each poster. Grandma helped to roll up the posters, secured each with a rubber band, and handed them back to the girls, providing each with a roll of tape.

"Hurry, now, and get these posters up," Grandma instructed. "*Lemonade Lilli* will be open for business in a couple of hours!"

The three girls tucked the posters under their arms and hurried to their bikes, chatting over each other about where to put up the posters. Lilli gave Grandma a quick hug of thanks before running back to the shop to help Grandpa and Larry paint her lemonade stand.

Chapter 10

When Lilli arrived at the shop, she saw that Grandpa had stirred up four cans of paint: red, green, yellow, and black. Grandpa had already started painting the top of the stand yellow.

"Why don't you grab that brush over there and paint your countertop green?" he suggested. "Your red cooler and yellow cups will look great on a green counter. It will make them stand out and look more appealing to your customers," he said with a wink.

Lilli laughed. She knew Grandpa was color-blind. "You're just saying what Larry said, aren't you?" she teased.

Grandpa let out a hearty laugh. "You know me too well, Lilli Bean!"

Larry walked over and showed Lilli his sketchpad. He pointed out each detail and described how it all worked together for the best visual presentation. Lilli wasn't sure if she understood everything Larry was telling her, but she was grateful that Larry had a talent for art, because she knew it would make her business better.

Lilli stood behind her stand and painted the countertop as Grandpa and Larry stayed on the other side working on the details. As she painted, she thought about everyone who had helped her and realized that she would never have been able to do all of this on her own. Lilli decided that if anyone ever needed her help with something in the future, she would do her best to help.

As Lilli finished her countertop, Larry stepped back and said, "There. Come on around and see."

Lilli walked around and stood next to Larry. "Wow!" Lilli exclaimed. "That looks great!" He had painted her business name in red on the top and added a sign on the bottom with the word "Lemonade" on it. Larry had also painted a giant lemon slice. It made her thirsty just looking at it! Lilli abruptly turned and gave her brother the best hug she knew how to give.

"It's a good thing I changed into my painting shirt before this hug," Larry said as he peeled Lilli and her wet green paintbrush off his chest.

"Oh, I'm sorry! I was so excited and grateful at the same time that I forgot to put my brush down!" Lilli looked sheepishly up at her brother.

"No worries, kiddo," Larry said as he tugged on her red ponytail. "That's why we call it a 'painting shirt.' "

"Larry!" Grandma called from the house. "Can you come and carry the lemonade cooler to the truck?"

"That's my cue," he said with a wink. "Apparently, I need to change my shirt, too!"

Lilli giggled as she started helping Grandpa clean up the paint and brushes.

"I'll finish cleaning this up." Grandpa said as he took the brush out of Lilli's hand. "You get cleaned up and find something colorful to wear."

"Thanks, Grandpa!" said Lilli with a smile, and then bounded toward the house.

Chapter 11

Lilli skipped into the kitchen after changing into her favorite pink shirt and yellow shorts, but before she could head out the door, Grandma stopped her.

"Here, this will make you look official." Grandma handed her a red apron with pockets in the front.

"Wow! This is great!" Lilli said as she quickly put it on. Grandma spun her around so that she could tie the strings in the back.

"Now you look ready for business, that's for sure," Grandma said with a smile. "Here is the bag of your supplies, and I'll carry the cups." Grandma handed Lilli a bag that contained a couple of kitchen towels, a money box, her sales log book, and several yellow crayons. "There are fifty one-dollar bills in your money box in case you need to make change. At the end of the day, you can pay me the fifty dollars back."

Lilli was grateful for Grandma's thinking; she had totally forgotten about making change! Fortunately, she knew how to do that. Grandma had taught her once when Lilli helped her with a bake sale and craft fair at school. "You start with the number of the total amount the customer is buying, then count up to the amount the customer gave you to pay for it," she had instructed. "For example, if someone is buying four dollars' worth of cupcakes and hands you ten dollars to pay for it, you start counting from the cost, which is four dollars, give the customer a dollar, which would make five dollars, and then give a five-dollar bill, which would equal ten dollars." At first Lilli was confused, but Grandma had practiced with her until she understood it. Now, Lilli really enjoyed figuring out change by carefully counting back the difference to each customer.

As they walked out to Larry's pickup, Lilli saw that Grandpa and Larry had just finished loading the lemonade stand into the back.

"There you go, Lilli Bean!" Grandpa called as he saw her approaching the truck. "You look like you are all set," he said with a grin.

Larry took the bags from Lilli and Grandma and organized everything in the back seat. Lilli quickly scrambled into the passenger seat as Larry slid in behind the wheel. As they rolled down the driveway, Lilli stuck her head out the window and smiled, waving enthusiastically at her grandparents. They waved back and Grandma called out, "Have fun!"

Chapter 12

They pulled into the dealership just as Mr. Barnham was coming out, dragging a huge round garbage can behind him. He smiled and waved when he saw Larry's truck and then gestured to a spot near the front door. Together, he and Larry unloaded Lilli's lemonade stand and placed it at just the right angle to be visible to customers going in and out of the building but not so close as to be in the way.

"Well," Mr. Barnham stated as he studied the lemonade stand, "that's a fine lemonade stand if ever I saw one."

Lilli beamed with pride. "My grandpa and Larry built it for me. I helped with the painting, but they did most of it. Larry is a really good artist, so he painted the pictures and my business name at the top."

Mr. Barnham studied the paint job more closely and said, "You did a fine job, Larry. When I need some advertising flyers made, I'll give you a call."

Larry set the big red cooler down, smiled, and said, "I'll look forward to that, Mr. Barnham. Thanks!"

Lilli studied her business setup closely. Everything looked ready to go. She turned to Larry and said, "Thanks for helping me, I really appreciate it!"

Larry gave her ponytail a quick tug and said, "Anything for you, kiddo. You have fun, and I'll be back to pick you up later." He gave a quick wave, climbed back into his truck, and took off.

Lilli turned to Mr. Barnham and asked, "I've been wondering about something. How do you go about paying the people who work for you?"

Mr. Barnham thought for a moment and said, "My employees are important to me because without them, I couldn't run my business very well. It would be too much for me to do."

Lilli understood, thinking about how much her grandpa, grandma, Larry, Lexie, Carole, and Kaylee had helped her. Even Mr. Barnham had helped her by allowing her to run her business on his property.

Mr. Barnham continued, "I treat them well and pay them well. If my employees are happy and enjoy working for me, they will most likely keep working for me for a long time and keep getting better at doing their jobs. In addition, if my employees are happy, then my customers will enjoy coming here and doing business with us. It's important to pay them a fair wage as well as bonuses for exceptional work. As far as how much to pay them, you need to know how much it costs to run your business and how much you need to make. From there, you can figure out what you can afford to pay people who help you."

"Thanks, Mr. Barnham. You have given me a lot to think about."

"You're going to have to think about it later, because it looks like your first customers have just arrived!" Mr.

Barnham stepped aside to reveal five of his employees heading outside to form a line in front of Lilli's lemonade stand.

Lilli hurried to get in position behind her stand and smiled at her first customer. He was a tall man with grease-stained overalls and a crooked smile.

"I sure am thirsty!" he said.

"You came to the right place!" Lilli replied, quickly retrieving a cup and filling it up. She set it on the counter in front of him and he handed her a large bill. Lilli set the money on the counter in front of her and began counting the difference, using the one-dollar bills her grandma had wisely put in her money box.

"I'm impressed!" he said as he pocketed the bills Lilli handed him. "Most kids nowadays don't know how to make change."

"My grandma taught me," Lilli said proudly.

"You have a smart grandma," he said with a nod. "And you were smart to learn how!" He tipped his hat to her and began to walk away. Suddenly, he turned back to her and said, "By the way, this is a FINE cup of lemonade! Just what I needed."

Lilli gave him a huge smile and called out, "Thank you!" She quickly grabbed one of her yellow crayons and colored in a lemon in her logbook before looking up and smiling at her next customer.

For the next hour, there was a steady stream of people, but not more than what Lilli could take care of. Some even told her that the reason they had come to her lemonade stand was that they had seen one of her posters in town. When Lilli heard this, she eagerly told her customers about her friends that had helped her and how Mother Kitty had decided to be their mascot.

The story always brought smiles and laughter from her customers, and Lilli reminded herself that what she had originally thought was a tragedy had turned out to be something positive. She was also reminded of what Mr. Barnham had said about the importance of making your customers happy.

Chapter 13

Lilli's attention was suddenly drawn toward the road when she heard several cars honking at each other. She started to feel nervous as she noticed there were a large number of vehicles preparing to turn into the dealership. *I need help!*

Lilli quickly found her cell phone and called Lexie.

"Hello?" Lexie answered.

"Lexie, thank goodness you answered your phone!" Lilli said with relief. "A bunch of cars just arrived and I need help!"

"We were already on our way to see you, so we'll be there in two minutes!" Lexie said, and then hung up.

A woman with white hair and a welcoming smile stepped forward to be Lilli's next customer. "A group of us just finished our dance class at the Senior Center, and someone mentioned there was a lemonade stand set up at the dealership. We all thought a cup of lemonade would be a refreshing treat! You must be Lilli?" she asked as she looked up at the *Lemonade Lilli* sign.

"Yes, that's me. I have just the thing for thirsty dancers! Would you like a cup of lemonade?"

"I would love one," she said with a smile. "Dancing does make you thirsty!"

It wasn't long before Lilli could hear the faint sound of bells ringing mixed with laughter. Her face split into a big smile as she saw her friends round the corner and turn into the parking lot. Lexie, Carole, and Kaylee parked their bikes and ran over.

"How's business?" Lexie asked.

"It's been great so far! A group of dancers from the Senior Center just arrived, and they are pretty thirsty!" Lilli said as she handed her next customer a cup.

"We were putting up posters and people started asking us what was going on," said Carole. "Of course, we told them, and then Kaylee suggested that they go tell everyone they knew about your lemonade stand!"

"My dad said that's called 'networking,' " Kaylee interjected. Kaylee's dad was a salesman and knew all about networking. "You just tell a few people about it and ask them to tell a few people, and before you know it, a lot of people know it!" Kaylee finished proudly.

Lilli noticed there was a long line forming and earnestly said, "Now I really need your help!"

The three girls scrambled behind the lemonade stand. "What would you like us to do?" asked Lexie.

"Lexie, you pour cups of lemonade. Carole, you hand the cup to the customer. Kaylee, you color in the lemons for each cup sold, and I'll collect the money!" Lilli ordered. The girls quickly took their places and soon had their assembly line system functioning smoothly.

Chapter 14

"Uh, Lilli?" Lexie said, her voice sounding a bit worried.

"What is it, Lexie?" Lilli turned to see Lexie with a panicked look on her face.

"We're running out of lemonade!" she said, the panic in her voice increasing with every word.

Oh no, what do I do? Lilli froze for a few seconds as she thought. *Call Grandma!* Lilli whipped out her cell phone from her apron pocket.

"Grandma! We are just about out of lemonade!" Lilli cried anxiously.

"No worries, Grandpa is on his way with some right now. I had an errand to run earlier, and when I drove by, I saw that you had a long line of customers. I told your grandpa that you would probably be running out soon, so I made more lemonade for you, and he offered to bring it to you. He should be there by now."

Lilli looked up and saw her grandpa pulling into the parking lot. "Oh, I see him! Grandma, you're the best!" Lilli said with relief. She hung up the phone and announced to her friends that her grandparents had come to the rescue!

"Hey there, Lilli Bean," Grandpa said as he lugged the heavy replacement cooler to the lemonade stand. "Your grandma thought you might be running low."

"She was right! I just got off the phone with her and she said you were on your way over. Your timing is perfect!" Lilli lifted the nearly empty cooler off the counter so Grandpa could replace it with the full one. "Thanks, Grandpa!"

"You're welcome, Lilli Bean," Grandpa said as he picked up the first cooler. "It looks like your line is about to get longer." Lilli looked up and saw a long line of cars and pickups streaming into the parking lot. She couldn't believe it! "My guess is that your brother had something to do with that." Grandpa gave her a couple pats on the back, and with a wink he said, "You better get back to work."

Lilli realized she had been frozen in place and forced herself to snap out of it. "Alright, girls, let's get to work!" The four girls quickly resumed their efficient system of customer service.

After they finished serving the Senior Center dance group, Larry approached and announced, "I found a few more customers for you!" He pointed to a large group of high school students heading their way. "A few of my friends were wondering what I had been doing all morning, so I told them about your lemonade stand business. They announced that they were suddenly very thirsty for lemonade, and apparently they told a few of their friends."

Lilli looked up at Larry and said, "You know, you're my favorite brother."

Larry laughed. "I'm your *only* brother."

"I don't care, you're still my favorite," she said with a grin.

Larry reached out and tugged on her ponytail. "Love you too, little sis. Now, how about some lemonade? I'm parched."

She took a cup of lemonade from Lexie and handed it to Larry. "This one's 'on the house!' " announced Lilli.

"Why, thank you," Larry said with a smile. "That is very kind of you."

"It was more kind of you to help me today," Lilli replied in a serious tone.

Larry winked at her and stepped aside so the next customer could approach the counter.

The girls continued to work as a team throughout the afternoon. When there weren't customers to serve, they cleaned up spilled lemonade, picked up trash that blew out of the garbage can—or didn't make it there in the first place—and updated the sales record book.

The stream of customers finally dwindled down to nothing, and at the end of the afternoon Mr. Barnham emerged from the building holding a small plastic bucket.

He smiled at the girls and said, "You all worked pretty hard this afternoon." The girls looked at each other and agreed that they felt they had. "And Lilli," Mr. Barnham continued, "you were right. We shared customers today! Your friends cleaned out my vending machine, and I think I sold at least three tractors I didn't expect to. I heard many great comments about how good your lemonade was but also, and more importantly, about what great customer service you provided. Everyone enjoyed talking to you girls, and were impressed with your business skills. One of my employees thought we should help you out even more and set this bucket on the counter inside." Mr. Barnham turned the bucket around to reveal a sign taped to it that said "Lemonade Tips."

All four girls' jaws dropped in surprise as Mr. Barnham placed the bucket on the lemonade stand counter in front of them. It was over half filled with bills of various amounts. He laughed at their surprised faces and said, "Go ahead, count it."

Lilli took the money out, sorted it on the counter, and began counting. There was $120 in the bucket! Lilli couldn't believe it. Her mind was racing, but then she had an idea. She divided the money into four piles and handed Lexie, Carole, and Kaylee $30 each. Lilli looked at her friends and said, "Thank you for helping me today. You earned it!"

The girls squealed with delight and began chatting about how they were going to spend their hard-earned cash. Lilli looked at Mr. Barnham and smiled, thinking about their earlier conversation and how important it was to treat employees well.

Mr. Barnham tipped his hat, smiled back, and said, "Well done, Lilli. I look forward to doing business with you again someday."

"Thank you, Mr. Barnham. I'll look forward to that, too!" Lilli turned back to her friends and said, "Let's pack up."

The girls pocketed their money and enthusiastically worked to clean and pack up. Lilli heard the familiar sound of Larry's pickup approaching and smiled as he and Grandpa slid out of the truck.

"How was business, Lilli Bean?" Grandpa asked.

"Better than I could have imagined!" Lilli said as she closed the bulging money box.

She reached into her apron pocket and handed Larry the remaining $30 from her tip bucket. "Thank you for helping me today, Larry."

Larry looked at her with surprise, but pocketed the cash with a smile and said, "Any time, kiddo."

She then turned to Grandpa, but before she could say anything, he put up his hands and said, "No need to pay me anything, Lilli Bean. A grandpa's job is to help, not get paid."

Lilli threw her arms around him and replied, "Thanks, Grandpa!"

"Let's get this stand loaded and head home. I'm sure Grandma has dinner ready." Lilli suddenly realized she was very hungry.

She turned to her friends and thanked them one more time before loading the pickup. The girls hopped onto their bikes, waved, rang their bike bells, and headed out. "See you soon!" Lexie called. Carole and Kaylee echoed Lexie's words and raced out of the parking lot.

Chapter 15

When they got home, Larry and Grandpa unloaded the stand and stored it in the shop as Lilli went inside. Grandma was sitting at the table reading the newspaper. She set the paper down and asked, "How did it go today?"

Lilli sat down next to her. "It was incredible! I had so many customers, and Mr. Barnham even had a lemonade tip bucket inside the dealership that I didn't know about until the end of the day."

"That was very nice of him."

"I divided the tip money by four and gave it to Larry, Lexie, Carole, and Kaylee, because they helped me so much today. Grandpa wouldn't let me pay him even though he helped me, too. Oh!" Lilli said, suddenly remembering their deal. "I owe you fifty dollars!" She opened her money box, counted out $50, and handed it to her grandma. "Thank you for all of your help, too, and for thinking of sending change money with me. I really needed it!" Lexi got up to give her grandma a hug.

"You worked hard today," Grandma noted.

"Running a business is a lot of work, but I had fun!" Lilli said as she plopped back down into her chair, realizing that her feet hurt from standing all afternoon.

Grandma laughed. "It is a lot of work, but it's important to remember your goals."

Lilli smiled, remembering her goal to make money. "Can you help me total my sales?"

"I sure can," she replied. Lilli retrieved her sales logbook and together the two of them began totaling each page.

"Impressive!" Grandma said as they counted the final page. "You really did well! Do you know what you're going to do with your money?"

"I have an idea, but I need to talk more about it with Grandpa," Lilli said thoughtfully.

"Why don't you go do that and let your grandpa and Larry know that dinner is ready?" Grandma said as she got up to attend to the food preparations.

Lilli got up and winced as her sore feet felt the weight of her body. She smiled as she remembered another of her grandpa's sayings: "It's not work unless it feels like it."

Lilli walked out to the farmyard and saw that Grandpa and Larry were talking by Larry's truck.

"What's up, Lilli Bean?" Grandpa asked as she approached.

"Grandma said that dinner is ready."

Larry jumped off the tailgate, patted his stomach, and said, "You don't have to tell me twice!" then headed to the house.

Grandpa noted Lilli's thinking face, bent down to pick her up, and set her on the tailgate. "What's on your mind?"

Lilli looked at her grandpa and said, "I have a lot of money now—more than I ever thought I'd have. I'm worried that I'll make a mistake with it."

Grandpa smiled and said, "Do you remember me talking about how it's important to save money, give money, and spend money?"

Lilli nodded. "Yes, I remember you saying that, but I don't know how much."

"I saw you give money to your friends and Larry. That was a good thing to do. Did you have something in mind that you wanted to buy?" Grandpa asked.

Lilli's face lit up. "Yes, I want to buy a brand new bicycle! I saw it at the bike shop last week and I can't stop thinking about it. Oh, Grandpa, it's the most beautiful lime-green color!"

Grandpa chuckled at her enthusiasm. "By the look of the crowd you had today, and the fact that I had to replenish your supply, I'm sure you have enough money to buy it."

Lilli grinned from ear to ear as she thought about riding her new bike. "Can we go buy it tomorrow?"

"I don't see why not," Grandpa replied. "What do you plan to do with the rest of your money?"

Lilli thought out loud, "Well, I gave some away, and I will be spending some tomorrow, so I guess I should save the rest?" She looked up at her grandpa for confirmation that she was making the right decision.

"Very good, Lilli Bean," Grandpa said approvingly. "Not only were you a success today running your very first business, but you also made good decisions with your money. The amount of money you give, spend, and save will always be up to you, but while you are young, I would recommend that you always save at least half of what you make. In the long run, if you can save more than that, you will be happy you did."

Lilli looked with relief at her grandpa and said, "I'm hungry. Can we go eat now?"

Grandpa laughed and lifted her off the tailgate. "My thoughts exactly, Lilli Bean!"

As they approached the front steps, Mother Kitty was there waiting for them. Lilli bent down to pet her and said, "Thanks for being my mascot today. Tomorrow I'll show you the new bike you helped me buy!" Mother Kitty purred loudly and rubbed up against Lilli's legs as she finally got the attention she had been looking for all day.

Coming Soon!
Book 1 – Fall, 2022

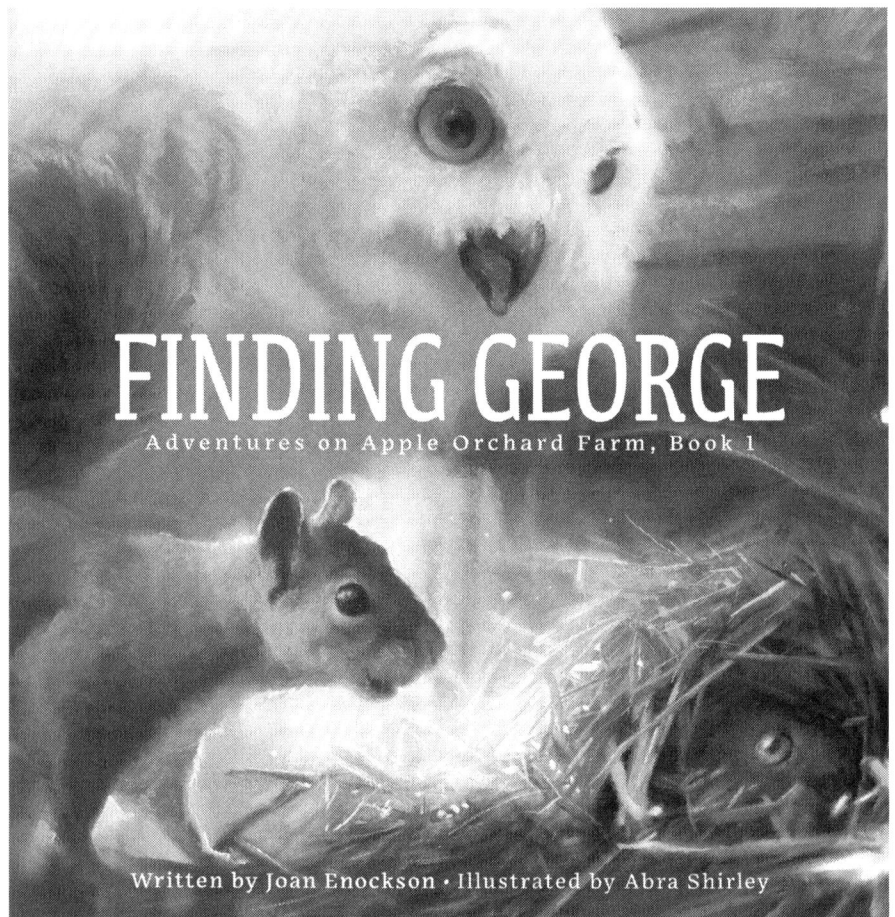

Orville, a snowy white owl, hears noises in the middle of the night.

He recruits his best friend, Simon the squirrel, to investigate. Join them as they seek to discover the answer to this mystery.

About the Author

Joan Enockson is an educator, musician, and author of children's books. Her books address social-emotional needs, friendship, problem-solving skills, citizenship, and patriotism.

She has experience teaching children of all ages in the public school system and strives to write in a style that intrigues young readers.

Joan holds an Associates degree in Office Administration, a Bachelor of Arts degree in Secondary Education specializing in Music, a Masters degree in Vocal Performance, and an endorsement to teach Talented And Gifted students.

Her stories are full of adventure and include life lessons that support 21st Century skills.

Tall Girl Publishing Publications

Children's Books

- *The Snail That Wanted To Hop!*
- *El caracol que queria saltar!*
    - Ages 1-8

- *Lemonade Lilli*
- *Limonada Lilli*
    - Ages 9-11

Record Keeping/Log Books/Notebooks

- *Tips From the Tractor-Notebook*
- *Garden Planner*
- *Home Maintenance*
- *Vehicle Maintenance*
- *Fish Tank Maintenance*
- *Motorcycle Maintenance & Trip Log*
- *Lemonade Stand Sales Log*
- *Family Vault*
- *Worship Notes*

Made in the USA
Monee, IL
31 July 2022